C000173712

Eccles

A Peculiarly Postmodern Piece

Doug Ingram

Lecturer in Old Testament
St John's College Nottingham

GROVE BOOKS LIMITED
RIDLEY HALL RD CAMBRIDGE CB3 9HU

Contents

Acknowledgments

My wife, Sue, has, as always, been hugely supportive in this project. She is my best critic and made invaluable comments which have resulted in a much more 'readable' booklet. In addition, Dawn Edginton and Sarah Giles read the manuscript and made helpful suggestions. The students at St John's College, Nottingham have, over a number of years, listened to the basic material presented here and interaction with them has been invigorating and challenging and has helped form my thinking on Ecclesiastes. Among these students I wish to thank especially David Cundill, Jill Needle, Rachel Wigram and Katie Windle. Thanks, too, are due to colleagues on the Grove Biblical series editorial group, especially Philip Jenson and Jo Bailey Wells.

A Note on Terms

Some scholars use the English term 'Ecclesiastes' to refer to this book of the Bible, while others use a transliteration of the Hebrew, 'Qohelet' (or 'Qoheleth', or 'Koheleth', or 'Coheleth'). I shall use 'Ecclesiastes' to designate the book and 'Qohelet' when I am referring to the main speaker in the book ('the Teacher' in the NIV and NRSV, traditionally 'the preacher'). I believe 'Qohelet' is a character in the book, and should be distinguished from the author of Ecclesiastes.

First Impression December 2004
ISSN 1365-490X
ISBN 1 85174 579 3

Introduction

1

'Ecclesiastes in all its ambiguity may hold the key to connecting with the culture of rock music; metaphor and symbol and meaninglessness all mingle just like a well crafted *Metallica* or *Nine Inch Nails* song. "Obsessed with death, Mr Cobain? So is Qohelet!"[1] It seems that in this one book there is more realism about the confusion and ambiguity of life than you could ever expect in the gospel.'

'Ambiguity and unanswerable questions, innocent suffering, joys and tragedies, glimpses of God and brasslike heavens, hope and despair, optimism and pessimism, wrestling and searching…such is the stuff of life and such is the stuff of Job and Ecclesiastes—what a relief!'

'Last year I found Ecclesiastes hard and not particularly helpful. This year I seem to be reading from a different perspective…Am I reading it differently because I am in a different "place" myself this year?'

The above is a selection of comments written by some of my students in the last few months. These quotations indicate something of what it is that sparked my interest in Ecclesiastes some twenty or so years ago. I was writing an undergraduate dissertation (on theodicy[2] in the Old Testament). As I studied the commentaries on Ecclesiastes I became fascinated by the diversity of their interpretations. As I studied Ecclesiastes itself my fascination grew as I discovered that such diversity seemed to be well supported by the text. The text, it seemed, was open to—perhaps even invited—different interpretations. The text, it seemed, was ambiguous—perhaps by design?

The text, it seemed, was ambiguous— perhaps by design?

In the next chapter I will give some examples to illustrate the diversity of interpretation, and the increasing acknowledgment by recent scholars that the book is open to different readings. I will then look at a key word (the word often translated 'vanity'), a key phrase ('under the sun') and a key passage in the book (1.4–11) to demonstrate their ambiguity. Next I will explain the conclusions I come to concerning such ambiguity, before, in the final chapter, exploring some of the implications that arise. This booklet (like Ecclesiastes) concludes with a brief epilogue.

2 Scholarly Interpretations of Ecclesiastes

What the Scholars Say about What Ecclesiastes Says

Commentators often quote two 19th century German scholars who present diametrically opposed views of Ecclesiastes. Delitszch describes it as 'The quintessence of piety,' while Heine thinks the book is 'The quintessence of scepticism.' In the middle of the 20th century an article appeared entitled, 'The Optimism of Koheleth,' while another had the title, 'The Pessimism of Ecclesiastes' and another again, 'The Peculiar Scepticism of Ecclesiastes.' Later that century two British scholars both described 'joy' as the key theme in the book[3] while for another 'despair' was the main message.[4] Among more recent commentators, one regards the book as positive, stating that its thesis is that 'life under God must be taken and enjoyed in all its mystery…holding firm, and positively accepting, life as God gives it.'[5] But another refers to 'the entire pessimistic, worldly thrust of the book,' where Qohelet musters 'evidence for the absurdity of life.'[6] One important commentary states that 'For Koheleth, joy is God's categorical imperative for man, not in any anaemic or spiritualized sense, but rather as a full-blooded and tangible experience,'[7] while another key work says, 'Life is profitless; totally absurd. This oppressive message lies at the heart of the Bible's strangest book.'[8]

It seems that Ecclesiastes has divided scholarly opinion as long as the book has been around. Even in the first century AD the Rabbis were divided over whether or not it should be included in the canon, and such disagreements continue among the most modern commentators. For example, a commentary published in 1997 states that 'The book of Ecclesiastes leaves no doubt about Qohelet's ultimate conclusion—everything is completely meaningless,'[9] while another published the same year maintains that 'He does not mean that everything is meaningless or insignificant, but rather that everything is beyond human apprehension and comprehension.'[10]

What the Scholars Say about What the Scholars Say about What Ecclesiastes Says

Most recent commentators acknowledge this kind of diversity of interpretation, and increasingly they recognize that such diversity has to do with whether the reader focuses more on the negative aspects of Ecclesiastes or on the positive parts. One scholar, for example, traces the 'variety of opinion' about the book from the first century and concludes,

> [The] division among the Rabbis throws into relief just where the problems of interpretation lie; in effect one side is saying that the orthodox and pious statements in the book modify and control the unorthodox, while the other side claims that the scepticism is of the essence of Qoheleth and remains over against the pious statements to be found there.[11]

Another argues similarly, stating,

> Depending on the relative weight placed by interpreters respectively on the negative or positive sides of statements [in Ecclesiastes], a whole range of assessments of Qoheleth's outlook, from one of extreme pessimism and despair to one of courageous faith and radiant optimism has been made by ancient and modern scholar alike.

He concludes, 'Whether he was a pessimist or an optimist, therefore, will remain a matter of opinion.'[12] My conclusion from studying Ecclesiastes in great detail and considering very carefully the range of interpretations of the book is that it readily lends itself to different readings. Thus, because the book is highly ambiguous, different readers (and even the same reader at different times in his or her life) will respond to the text differently because of what they bring to the text. I think the commentator is correct who says, 'It may be that in the last resort Qoheleth is a mirror which reflects the soul of the interpreter.'[13] A very recent book argues similarly, saying, 'It is still common for readers to attribute the difficulties of Ecclesiastes entirely to the text itself. Our research has shown that this perplexity is as much a product of the reader as it is of the text.'[14] But, to my mind, the ambiguous nature of Ecclesiastes is best captured in these words from a study published in 2001 which adopts a decidedly postmodern perspective on the book:

> The Book of Ecclesiastes confronts the critic with intricate reading problems that constantly generate a sense of ambiguity in the reader…The reader is left suspended in a state of literary limbo regarding the text's final meaning. An ambiguous text is characterized by the enduring and resolute presence of multiple interpretations which seem equally justified.[15]

My contention is, then, that Ecclesiastes is fundamentally ambiguous *by design*. What I will do now is to illustrate that ambiguity. Then I will explore what implications there might be for Christian readers of a biblical book which is open to a variety of interpretations in the way that I believe Ecclesiastes to be.

3

A Key Word, a Key Phrase and a Key Passage

'Ambiguity of ambiguities,' said Qohelet, 'Ambiguity of ambiguities, all is ambiguous'

The word translated in the NRSV as 'vanity' (*hebel* in Hebrew) is clearly a key word in Ecclesiastes. It is used some 38 times in the book's 12 chapters (although it is used much more in the first two chapters than elsewhere). The phrase 'vanity of vanities' occurs in 1.2 and again in 12.8 and seems to function as something of a 'motto' for the book. In fact, this phrase is one of the best known parts of the book, having passed into common English usage even though most people do not know where it came from. It appears to encapsulate the repeated phrases 'all is vanity' and 'this too is vanity' in Ecclesiastes. One commentator says, 'The function of the motto is to guide the reader toward a proper interpretation of Qohelet's words;'[16] and another writes, 'The book's motto is a thesis that we can expect to see validated by the following monologue, and which by this expectation controls the way we read.'[17] These and many other commentators see this motto as the crucial element in the book, and how we understand the word *hebel* is therefore very important. A recent short book on Ecclesiastes captures the view of most scholars when it argues that 'any reading of Ecclesiastes is based on one's estimation of this key word.'[18]

But therein lies the problem. Figure 1 lists some of the words used to translate *hebel*, and it is clear that if this is a (if not *the*) key word in the book which 'guides the reader' and 'controls the way we read,' very different readings will be achieved depending on how this word is understood. Thus to say that everything is 'absurd' or 'meaningless' is rather different from describing things as 'transient' or 'enigmatic.' If this is such an important word which has so major a bearing on our understanding of the book, the wide range of translations and interpretations of the word must raise serious questions about

Words used to render the Hebrew word *hebel*:				
absurd	breath	emptiness	enigmatic	futile
incomprehensible	ironic	meaningless	mysterious	smoke
temporary	transient	unknowable	useless	vanity
vapour	wind	worthless		

Figure 1

the interpretation of the book as a whole. These words from a popular-level commentary on Ecclesiastes capture something of this:

> How is it possible for one small book to generate such opposite and contradictory theories about its meaning? One important reason is the ambiguity of the thematic word *hebel*…Ecclesiastes has been understood in radically different ways by readers in part because the thematic metaphor 'all is *hebel*' is fundamentally ambiguous.[19]

This crucial word, then, rather than providing the key to the interpretation of the book, seems to leave a gap to be filled in. Thus in a commentary on Ecclesiastes published this year we read, 'The motto of the book of Qoheleth is indeed "misunderstandable in the highest degree." Its point in regard to what follows seems to lie, however, in its very openness and ambiguity.'[20] We end up being caught in a 'hermeneutical spiral' where the meaning of the word *hebel* depends on how we understand the book as a whole, but the meaning of the book as a whole is built up by our understanding of such words as *hebel*. And it turns out that other important words in the book ('toil,' 'gain,' 'good,' 'bad') are also ambiguous, with commentators explaining them quite differently depending on their readings of the book as a whole.

The origin of *hebel* is uncertain, but it appears to be an onomatopoeic word (that is, it sounds like what it means) meaning 'breath, vapour,' though it is rarely used in the Old Testament with this meaning. Other semitic languages have cognate words with the same meaning. They, like biblical Hebrew, use the word in its literal sense and in a figurative sense. In the Old Testament *hebel* seems to be used figuratively in two ways, of what is ephemeral or transient (or something similar), and of what is vain or useless (or something similar). It is often used to describe idols or false gods. It rather seems that its use in Ecclesiastes is like its basic meaning—it is like a vapour in that when you try to pin it down and capture its essence, you discover that it has slipped through your fingers and there is nothing left to hold on to. So we might well say that 'ambiguity of ambiguities,' while it certainly is not an appropriate translation of the motto, does give a sense of the slippery nature of the key word *hebel* which is so important for understanding the strange yet fascinating book of Ecclesiastes.

What is Done 'Under the Sun'

Another phrase from Ecclesiastes which is well-known (and again many people do not know where it comes from) is 'under the sun.' This expression does not occur anywhere else in the Old Testament, although the apparently synonymous phrase, 'under heaven,' which is used three times in Ecclesiastes, is found elsewhere. 'Under the sun' is clearly a key expression in the book of

Ecclesiastes, occurring 29 times. It, too, is ambiguous, but in a rather different way. Unlike *hebel*, the translation of the phrase is uncontested. The difficulty here is how to *interpret* the phrase. One scholar explains the ambiguity thus:

> There are two ways in which this phrase might be used, restrictive and expansive. In the first, the purpose of the phrase would be modestly to restrict the application of Qohelet's observations only to the world, so as to exclude other spheres that are beyond human knowledge. 'Under the sun' then would be used to distinguish the field of observation from the non-human spheres of reality. In this case, Qohelet would be holding out the possibility of a different situation elsewhere, *ie*, in the heaven or the underworld…The meaning of the phrase is the same in the second possible use, but its function is different. In this case, Qohelet's purpose would be to emphasize the breadth of his observations, claiming that such-and-such is true in the entire world 'under the sun,' not just in part of it.[21]

He acknowledges that the first sense is 'the traditional understanding of the phrase,' which 'makes Qohelet out to be pious and modest in his claims and even hints at hopes for a better life above and beyond this one.' But he argues that 'The inclusive function is more likely,' explaining, 'Since most of the facts that Qohelet observes "under the sun" can hardly be imagined to exist in any other domain but human life, there is no need for him to exclude other domains of reality.'[22] However, a number of commentators over the years have taken the opposite view. A recent commentary states, 'Qohelet thus restricts his remarks to terrestrial human activity and work…Qohelet's frequent use of the phrase under the sun highlights the restricted scope of his inquiry.'[23]Another argues similarly, saying that Qohelet 'will conclude that there is no lasting benefit here on earth, by which he may be suggesting that there is one beyond this life.'[24]

It makes a considerable difference to the way Ecclesiastes is understood whether the reader believes that Qohelet is undertaking an exhaustive study of *everything*, or understands Qohelet to be taking account *only* of what happens on earth while allowing that things may be different in another realm. Matters are further complicated by the use of 'under heaven' three times (1.13; 2.3; 3.1). This raises the question why a different term is used just these few times, and whether or not readers should understand it simply as a synonym. Moreover another expression is used four times which might also be synonymous: (up)on earth (5.2; 8.14, 16; 11.2). In 8.14–17 'under the sun' and 'on earth' alternate, which may indicate that they are synonymous. But perhaps 5.2 is the most significant verse in this discussion: 'Never be rash with your mouth, nor let your heart be quick to utter a word before God, for God is in heaven, and you upon earth; therefore let your words be few.' It may be that this is a deliberate play on Deuteronomy 4.39, which admonishes: 'Acknowledge today and take heart that the Lord is God in heaven above and on the earth beneath; there is no other.' Thus Ecclesiastes emphasizes that '(up)on earth' is the human realm, while 'in heaven' is the divine realm. Might this at least hint that 'under the sun'/'under heaven'/'(up)on earth' refer specifically to the human sphere as opposed to where God is? Perhaps, but the text here in Ecclesiastes is actually ambiguous, allowing for different readings of the key phrase 'under the sun.'

Mixing in Hermeneutical Circles

I move on now from considering a key ambiguous word in Ecclesiastes (*hebel*, 'vanity'), through discussion of a key ambiguous phrase ('under the sun'), to consider a key ambiguous passage. Because 'vanity of vanities' and 'under the sun' are such well-known phrases, it might have been good to look next at the famous poem in 3.1–8 (known to many in the words of the song, 'To everything/turn, turn, turn/there is a season/turn, turn, turn, turn./A time to…' and so on). This passage would have suited my purposes here very well, as a comparison of two commentaries published in 1987 illustrates. One commentator writes about this poem, 'An arbitrary deity shapes human lives, allowing some persons to participate in pleasure and preventing others from doing so.'[25] The other describes the author's conviction 'that creation is marked by an orderliness which takes its origin in the divine plan and will.'[26] Of course, we know that the meaning of a word, phrase or passage should not be determined in isolation from its context, so perhaps a consideration of the broader context of this time poem will help. But here again the commentators disagree. For example, one writes,

> The key to the meaning Koheleth attaches to [3.1–8] is to be found in the following verses (9–15), which represent the conclusions to which he comes…a) all acts are predetermined and all human activity is therefore useless…b) all events, even those which man regards as calamities, have their place in God's plan. What oppresses Koheleth is that man is given no glimpse of that meaning.[27]

But another states, 'Thank God for providence. If we read verses 1–8 through the lens of verses 11–15 this becomes the dominant thought. God presides in love over all the circumstances of our lives.'[28]

However, fruitful as such a study might be, I intend to look instead at the poem in 1.4–11. The reason for this choice is that it is the first passage in Ecclesiastes after the introductory verses 1.1–3, and it establishes patterns which can be found throughout the book. There are at least three ways in which this passage is ambiguous. Firstly, it uses ambiguous words at important points—at the beginning, in the middle and at the end! Secondly, it is unclear how the two halves of the poem relate to each other. And finally, the place of this poem in (and especially at the beginning of) the book as a whole raises a number of questions.

The following section will be much easier to follow if you keep the text open in front of you while you read! I offer a couple of different translations of these verses further below.

Ambiguous Words

The very first word in 1.4 (*dor*, 'generation') is ambiguous. One commentator explains the issue in this way: 'The word *dor*, an appropriate choice because of its ambiguity, suggests both nature and people. The primary sense here is probably the former: the generations of natural phenomena.'[29] Many commentators acknowledge this ambiguity, but most choose the latter sense of the word. In fact, following on directly from 1.3, the latter sense is most likely to be the reader's initial impression, but this may well be modified when the following verses relate to the natural realm—and perhaps modified again in light of vv 8–10! Verse 11, as we shall see, then throws the whole question up in the air again.

The ambiguity continues throughout the verse. 'Goes' (*holek*) and 'comes' (*ba'*) could indicate the 'going' and 'coming' of natural eras, or the 'dying' and 'being born' of human generations—a sense they have elsewhere in Ecclesiastes (see 5.14, 15; 6.4) and the Old Testament. 'The earth' (*ha'arets*) often refers to the physical earth (or the land, as in, the 'promised land'), but it might also indicate the human world—a sense it may have elsewhere in Ecclesiastes (5.8; 7.20; 10.16, 17) and the Old Testament. Indeed, one scholar argues, 'The key to understanding this verse lies in recognizing that *ha'arets* here does not mean the physical earth, but humanity as a whole—"le monde" rather than "la terre."'[30] Moreover, the conjunction rendered 'but' in the NRSV may either function conjunctively, 'and,' or disjunctively, 'but,' so that the second half of the verse either confirms the first half or stands in contrast to it.

'Forever' (*'olam*) is ambiguous (at least to modern readers) because it is uncertain if it conveys the sense of 'eternity' in anything like the way we understand the concept today. Commentators are divided on this question as well. This is a big issue in terms of its use in 3.11 which the NIV renders, 'He [God] has made everything beautiful in its time. He has also set eternity in the hearts of men; yet they cannot fathom what God has done from beginning to end.' The NRSV renders *'olam* here with 'a sense of past and future,' which is certainly an interpretation rather than a translation. However, this is an important point for interpretation of the whole book—just what did God place in human hearts, and why?

The ambiguity of *dor* ('generation') in 1.4 is picked up again in verse 11. Here the phrases 'the people of long ago' (one word in Hebrew, *ri'sonim*) and 'people yet to come' (*'aharonim*) could indicate either people who come before and after or things that come before and after. Both senses of the words are found elsewhere in the Old Testament and the commentators disagree on which it should be here. Thus at the beginning and end of the passage it is unclear whether humanity or nature is being referred to—or, perhaps, both.

And, indeed, the same ambiguity occurs at the centre of the passage. 1.4–11 falls into two halves. The first half of the passage describes cycles in nature. The second half relates these cycles to repetition in the human arena. At the centre of the passage we find the words, 'All things are wearisome' (NRSV). The word rendered 'things' may be understood abstractly as 'things,' and taken as a reference to the natural cycles in the preceding verses, or it may be translated 'words,' and linked with the human activities in the following section. The word rendered 'wearisome' is translated in various ways by the commentators as weary, wearisome or busy. It could fit with an interpretation focusing either on natural cycles or on human activities. It could also give the verse a decidedly negative tinge—or be read quite positively.

Relationship Between the Two Halves of the Passage
One commentator says of the first half of the passage, 'This poem characterizes nature as an endless round of pointless movement,'[31] while another argues that 'These examples are not intended to show the futility of these phenomena, but only their regularity…the reader is implicitly invited to regard their activity with wonder and admiration.' Of the second half of the passage one scholar writes, 'As in the natural world, so too in human life there is no true change, only dreary repetition,'[32] while another describes it as 'a shout of joy: behind the ephemeral moment shines eternal permanence.'[33]

There is a balance between the three natural elements in the first half of the passage (sun, wind and water), and the three human activities in the second half (speech, sight and hearing). But either half may be read more or less positively or negatively, and the relationship between the two halves of the passage is also ambiguous. Thus the constancy of God's creation may be being affirmed throughout. Or the tedium of the endless repetition in nature may be being likened to the unending and unchanging cycles of human generations. Or the constancy of nature may be being contrasted with the brevity of a human life which achieves nothing new or of lasting value and is soon forgotten.

Actually, the ambiguity at this level reflects reality—the cycles of nature are observable phenomena to which people respond in their own way. On the one hand, the provision of nature can be gratefully accepted, and, in the best traditions of scientific research, its predictability can be utilized to best effect. On the other hand, one can succumb to despair at the monotony of nature that fails to provide for the inexhaustible greed of humankind which seeks gratification of desires beyond the grasp of life 'under the sun.' This is a key element of how I think the book of Ecclesiastes works and an important aspect of human life—the pessimist will find plenty to moan about, the optimist will find plenty to rejoice in. In an effort to illustrate the ambiguity of this passage, I offer two readings of the text in parallel in the boxes below, one decidedly negative, the other more positive.

The Relationship of 1.4–11 to the Rest of the Book

1.4–11 bears no obvious link either with what precedes in 1.1–3, or with what follows in 1.12–2.3 (which I believe to be the next section of the book). Indeed, 1.12 looks rather as though it was intended as the introduction to Ecclesiastes, which raises questions about the role played by the supposed 'introduction' (as indeed it is presented by many commentators) in 1.1–11. Moreover, 1.12–2.3 serves as a kind of overture to the book by giving a taster of important issues

---

Reading 1: To Be Read in a Depressed and Tedious Fashion!

1 The words of Qohelet, David's son and king in Jerusalem.
2 'Utterly absurd,' says Qohelet, 'Utterly absurd—everything is absurd.
3 What *possible* benefit can a person get from the toil at which people everywhere struggle?
4 People just come and go. But the earth endures for ever.
5 The sun rises and the sun sets—then it wearily returns to its place to rise all over again.
6 And the wind—it goes to the south, then goes round to the north. It goes round and round…and round…and round endlessly.
7 And the rivers—well they flow into the sea, but they never manage to fill the sea because they too are in an endless cycle.
8 Everything is tired of it—and people have nothing to say. They're never happy with what they see, nor satisfied with what they hear,
9 because what happens in the future will just be a repeat of what happened in the past, and what is done in the future will be the same as what's been done in the past. There's nothing really new anywhere.
10 Sometimes people say, "Look, this is new." But actually it's been around for ages:
11 people just don't remember those who went before, nor will they be remembered by the people who come after them.'

---

that will be addressed in greater depth later on. 1.4–11, by contrast, is notable for its lack of key words, phrases and themes that are characteristic features of Ecclesiastes, and also for its distinctiveness in terms of style and grammar.

However, this section does establish a pattern which is followed throughout the book, more or less explicitly. The first half of the passage pictures the way things are on earth; the second half explores the implications of this for human life—in a somewhat ambiguous way so that readers are forced to draw their own conclusions. Throughout the book the author makes observations about life 'under the sun,' then draws some conclusions from these observations. (Indeed, there is a *trend* from more observation at the start of the book to more conclusions towards the end. This is why the word *hebel* and other key words occur in a higher concentration in the early chapters. There is, though, a degree of intermingling of observations and conclusions throughout.) It is my contention that the conclusions drawn are generally rather ambiguous so that the reader is constantly required to fill in gaps in order to establish the meaning of what is being said. This, I believe, is an important aspect of Qohelet's reflections on life—and also on death, explicitly a few times, implicitly often.

Reading 2: To Be Read Positively and with Enthusiasm!

1 The words of Qohelet, David's son and king in Jerusalem.
2 'Vapour of vapours,' says Qohelet, 'Vapour of vapours, everything is a vapour.
3 What real profit is there for people from all their work at which they strive so hard…in *this* life?
4 People die…but then others are born. And the world continues forever:
5 The sun rises and sets, then eagerly rises again.
6 The wind goes to the south and to the north and goes round and round, and continues to go round.
7 And the rivers flow to the sea, but they never run dry because the water returns to flow all over again.
8 Words are such a bind, aren't they! They just can't capture it all. Nor can our eyes or ears take it all in.
9 But in fact there's nothing totally new in this life, because what happens in the future has happened in the past, and what is done in the future has been done in the past.
10 People sometimes say, "Look, *this* is new!" But, no, it will have happened sometime in the past.
11 People just don't remember what happened in the past—and people in the future won't remember either!'

The responses of the commentators to 1.4–11 is revealing. For the most part those who take a more positive view of the book as a whole tend to see in this section an affirmation of the order which God has established in nature (and they generally read 3.2–8 in a similar fashion). But those who read the book negatively tend to view the passage as complaint about the futility of the endless cycles of nature and human life. This pattern is repeated throughout the book—on many occasions the interpretations offered are diametrically opposed as some commentators draw out the positive threads and others point up the negative aspects. In each case one may find one or other reading more convincing, but the point is that for the most part the positive and negative readings are well-grounded in the text itself. It seems that, depending on one's perspective, it is possible on many occasions to sustain a positive or a negative reading of passages in Ecclesiastes depending on what is 'foregrounded' and what is 'marginalized.' Like Rubin's figure-ground discrimination problem (figure 2), both the 'light' and the 'dark' reading are present. If the 'lighter' elements are marginalized, the text produces a 'dark' reading. If the 'darker' elements are marginalized, the text produces a 'light' reading. The difficulty is that whichever reading is adopted, whether a more positive one or a negative one, there are other elements in the text which cannot readily be ignored. There are other voices in Ecclesiastes crying out to be heard.

Figure 2:
Rubin's figure-ground discrimination problem. What do *you* see?

In the next chapter I will explain the conclusions I come to in light of the ambiguous nature of key words, phrases and passages in the book of Ecclesiastes and the diversity of interpretations among scholars (and others) generated by this ambiguity.

My Conclusion—'Such is Life!' 4

When I first took an interest in Ecclesiastes as an undergraduate, nearly twenty years ago, 'Ecclesiastes Studies' was something of a quiet backwater.

It was not to remain so. Over the past 15 or so years a large number of commentaries and other books and articles—not to mention doctoral theses, a good indication of current interest—have appeared on this book. But why? Part of the explanation is probably that the previous lack of interest generated a vacuum which had to be filled! But the interest is not restricted to those in the academic arena who might be aware that such a vacuum even existed. The book has attracted considerable popular interest as well. I believe that much of the interest arises from Ecclesiastes' particular appeal to those affected, all be it unconsciously, by postmodernity. Society today, as never before, is aware of the ambiguous nature of the world. It is no longer satisfied with a previous generation's 'metanarratives' (which sought to provide all the answers), nor indeed does it seek any overarching worldview to give structure to life. In this post-structuralist, deconstructionist world order, certainty and security seem to be things of the past. In modern society ambiguity was marginalized in favour of producing coherent meaning. Postmodern society is content to live with ambiguity, and to permit (and even to encourage) a plurality of different voices and meanings.

Ecclesiastes was a problem for a previous 'scientific' generation (using 'scientific' in a popular sense—I am sure many scientists would object!). It refused to fit into a neat mould. Whatever consistent meaning was discerned in the book was only given voice by pushing to the margins other voices crying out to be heard. Such plurality, such discord, such lack of consistent meaning, such unstructuredness—such ambiguity appeals to a postmodern reader and accords well with the world as seen through postmodern eyes.

It is precisely this ambiguous nature of life 'under the sun' that is captured by the ambiguity in Ecclesiastes. It has often been suggested that whatever else the author of Ecclesiastes is, that author is at least a realist, and a key element in that realism is the portrayal by means of ambiguous text of a world which is itself subject to hugely varied interpretation. One scholar takes a first step towards acknowledging this aspect of the book when he says,

> Qohelet bares his soul in all its twistings and turnings, ups and downs, and he invites readers to accompany him in pursuit of fresh discovery. But the contradictions suggest more than the result of time's passage. They express the ambiguities of daily existence.[34]

Another goes somewhat further, arguing that when we read Ecclesiastes, we 'enter an extremely ambiguous universe, in which we can never be sure we have fathomed the author's intention.'[35] The same might be said of life under the sun. It, too, is extremely ambiguous, and people can rarely (if ever?) be sure they have fathomed its Author's intention—however hard they may seek, however wise they may be, however much they may claim to know. Take, for example, the cycles of nature described in 1.4–7. Are they dependable phenomena which provide an element of security and predictability to life, or are they part of a monotonous cycle of endless repetitions from which there is no escape?

According to 3.1–8, everything under the sun has its time. Are **people** then but pawns in a cosmic chess game over which they have no real control (as 7.13, 14 seem to assert) and whose rules they can never fully comprehend (as 8.17 may imply)? Or are they free to explore the limits and limitations of life (as Qohelet does throughout: 1.13, 17; 2.1, 3, 10, 12; 7.25; 8.9; 9.1) and express and enjoy themselves within these necessary restrictions (as perhaps is advised in the 'calls to enjoyment' in 2.24; 3.12–13, 22; 5.18–19; 8.15; 9.7–9; 11.9–10)?

Is **work** (or 'toil'—the word is ambiguous) a necessary evil to provide the means for survival and what little pleasure people can glean in the few days of life available to them (as in 2.18–23)? Or is it given to enrich life and provide creative activity (as may be indicated in 2.24; 5.17 and 9.9)?

Is **wisdom** a benefit which enables its possessor to more fully appreciate the complexities of the world and to live a more fulfilling life as a result (as suggested by verses such as 2.13–14a, 24; 7.11–12, 19; 8.1; 9.17–18; 10.2–12)? Or is it an extra burden which gives greater insight into the injustices and anomalies of life, but which does not provide any ultimate return (which seems to be argued in 1.18; 2.14b–16, 21; 7.13–18; 8.16–17; 9.10–11, 13–16; 10.1)?

Is **death** a blessed release from life under the sun (4.2)? Or is it the final irony which casts its shadow over all the pleasures of life (as 9.10 suggests and perhaps is implied in 11.8; 12.7–8)? Or is it the supreme injustice because it takes no account of good or evil (as Qohelet complains in 2.14b–16; 9.2–3)? Or is it simply one of the necessary limits within which people have to operate (as may be intended in 3.2; 11.8 and perhaps 12.7)?

In an ambiguous world people are confronted by endless data which they read differently (not only from other people, but also at different times in their own lives) according to the interpretative strategy they bring to bear upon it. The writer of Ecclesiastes observes this world very carefully and records these observations in language that captures the world's ambiguous nature.

Patterns in Ecclesiastes, Patterns in Life

Not only is the ambiguous nature of the text of Ecclesiastes a reflection of life under the sun, so too are the patterns that can be observed in the book. There undoubtedly are patterns and structures in Ecclesiastes, which tempt the reader to seek the one overall pattern that explains the way the book is put together. Many scholars have yielded to the temptation, some claiming to have discerned the definitive structure.[36] Others agree with the oft-quoted words of Delitzsch, 'All attempts to show, in the whole, not only oneness of spirit, but also a genetic progress, an all-embracing plan, and an organic connection, have hitherto failed, and must fail.'[37] This, too, reflects life under the sun—here too there are patterns and structures which tease people into trying to find the solution that explains it all, to search for 'grand narratives.'

One of the features of postmodernity is the realization that no such solution is to be found; one of the features of my reading of Ecclesiastes is the claim that no such solution to the structure of Ecclesiastes is to be found. We can certainly discover trends in the book, for example a development from first person to second person address, or from observations about what happens under the sun to statements about the limitations of human knowledge, but none of these provides a sufficient explanation of the book's overall structure. Similarly, trends can be discerned in the world, for example that those who act wisely or righteously tend to benefit in some way as a result (thus 8.12b–13; and most of ch 10), or that power is frequently on the side of an oppressor while the oppressed have no-one to comfort them (4.1; 5.7), but none of these trends provides a sufficient governing principle for life.

We can discover structures within Ecclesiastes, but any attempt to structure the whole book in similar fashion is ultimately frustrated. Attempts are still made, and will no doubt continue to be made, to find the structure of Ecclesiastes, but any overall structure to the book involves some degree of manipulation of the text to make it fit a particular pattern. Similarly, life under the sun eludes our efforts to discern an overall pattern in which everything has its appropriate place. No matter how simple or sophisticated our philosophy, there will always be those aspects of life that defy explanation and refuse to fit our scheme. Of course, such aspects of life (and Ecclesiastes) may be pushed to the margin, but it is only as we allow the voices from the margin to speak and to challenge our own presuppositions that we truly begin to understand the world (and Ecclesiastes) in all its plurality and ambiguity.

It may be argued that there is one certainty both for the writer of Ecclesiastes and in the world—that death is the end of life under the sun. But even this is ambiguous. The text opens (after the introductory verses 1.1–3) with (an ambiguous) reference to the coming and going of generations (1.4, 11), and ends (in 12.1–7, before the epilogue in 12.9–12) with a description of approaching death. But the final words of this description could hint at the possibility of something beyond death, a hint that might also be found in 3.21, but stands in some tension with 9.10. Moreover, at least in the canonical form of the book (and, I would maintain, also by the author's design; it is not an editorial addition as most scholars maintain) there is an epilogue that takes the reader beyond Qohelet's study of life—and death—under the sun. Qohelet ('the Teacher' in the NRSV) whose words are recorded in 1.2–12.8, is now described in the third person, and also in the past tense—Qohelet was a wise person, who taught the people knowledge and sought to find pleasing words. In the epilogue readers are taken beyond the world described by the person (or, more probably, persona) Qohelet so that they are privy to the perspective of the omniscient author, who then addresses the readers directly in the imperatives of the second half of the epilogue. The confident assertion with which the epilogue—and the book—closes, that God will bring all deeds into judgment, raises again the question whether life 'under the sun' is all there is. Qohelet examined thoroughly every aspect of this world, but perhaps—and here lies the final great ambiguity of the book—the author finally takes the readers beyond Qohelet's world, beyond the realm under the sun where everything is characterized by *hebel*. The epilogue to Ecclesiastes might then serve a similar purpose to the prologue to Job. The prologue to the book of Job takes its readers outside the world Job knows and gives them privileged information to which Job, his three companions and Elihu do not have access. However, two crucial differences should be noted. Firstly, God features as a speaking character in Job but is notably silent in Ecclesiastes. Secondly, Job commences with explicit acknowledgment of another realm but Ecclesiastes gives only the faintest ambiguous hints that there may be something beyond life under the sun.

So, in conclusion, different people with different presuppositions 'read' the world, life and death differently and come to different conclusions about its 'meaning' and the intentions of its 'Author' (if they accept that such an Author exists). Indeed, the readers and commentators of this particular 'text' have throughout known history disagreed, and will no doubt continue to disagree, about its Author, its setting, its structure and its meaning. It seems to me that 'such is life.' It seems to me also that such is the book of Ecclesiastes.

Let us begin to explore the implications of this for our reading of Ecclesiastes and of the Old Testament, and for living as Christians in the 21st century.

Is this 'The End of the Matter'? 5

I have tried in this study to highlight some of the textual ambiguity of Ecclesiastes, and to explore how this captures something of the ambiguity of the (text of) the world we inhabit.

This raises a number of questions which deserve further consideration:

- Is it likely that the author of Ecclesiastes intended it to be as ambiguous as I have made out?
- Why might the author have produced such an ambiguous book?
- Am I reading Ecclesiastes too much as a child of the postmodern era?
- Is the approach to reading I have adopted here appropriate for the reading of Holy Scripture?
- To what extent ought we as Christians to emphasize certainty over ambiguity?
- How might we as Christians cope with a world full of ambiguity and uncertainty?

Before giving some brief responses to these questions (which I will then leave the reader to think about further!), I wish to make some more positive comments about the book of Ecclesiastes. I do not think it is simply an ambiguous morass in which readers wade around grabbing onto any 'meaning' they happen to find floating by. The book is not just a 'mirror which reflects the soul of the interpreter,' which I noted above is the view of one scholar. Perhaps it is more like a highly polished stained glass window which, depending on where the light is focused, will reveal something of the reader's reflection, might also reveal something of the author's (or Author's) intention lying behind it, but which also bears its own image that continues to be a crucial element in how it is read. Even without the epilogue, Ecclesiastes is not a disinterested representation of an ambiguous world—were such a thing possible. A crucial element in the interpretative strategy that the author brings to bear on the 'text' of the ambiguous world explored in the book is that there is a God.

Ecclesiastes is certainly not a 'Godless' book—God features often, a total of 40 times in the 12 chapters. Moreover, there are three main characteristics of this God to which attention is drawn (and which account for 39 out of the 40 explicit references to God in the book). None of these can the author have discerned by simple observation of the world—this is part of his worldview which he holds by faith.

Firstly, God gives. 13 times (or 14 if the 'one shepherd' in 12.11 refers to God) the verb 'to give' is used with God as subject (1.13; 2.26, 26; 3.10, 11, 13; 5.18, 19, 19; 6.2; 8.15; 9.9; 12.7). On three further occasions God's giving is described without using the specific verb (2.24; 5.20; 9.7), and once God's *not* giving is referred to, again without using the specific verb 'to give.' What God gives does not always seem to be 'good' for sure (see, for example, 7.14), but there is a repeated exhortation throughout the book to enjoy the good things that God gives (see 2.24, 26; 3.12–13; 5.18–19; 8.15; 9.9). It seems to me (and others!) that there is a very positive message which comes across clearly in Ecclesiastes—rather than striving to understand and control life, accept the good things which come your way as a gift of God. Most of the positive parts of the book are set in the context of what God gives, and if God's gifts are accepted as such, rather than sought as our right, our whole outlook will be different.

> *If God's gifts are accepted as such, rather than sought as our right, our whole outlook will be different*

Secondly, God acts. The verb 'to do, make' is used 11 times in connection with God (3.11, 11, 11, 14, 14; 7.13, 14, 29; 8.17; 11.5, 5). But we are also informed that God 'seeks' (3.15), 'tests' (3.18), and 'judges' (3.17; 11.9; 12.14). Perhaps the reference to 'your creator' in 12.1 could be included in this category. It may well be that it is beyond human ability to comprehend what God does (3.11–14; 8.17; 9.1–2; 11.1–6), but Ecclesiastes portrays a God who is actively involved in the world that God has created. It is notable that many commentators recommend excising 3.17 because it does not fit with their negative reading of the book and seems to stand in stark contrast with the preceding verse. However, the juxtaposition of these verses illustrates well Qohelet's belief in a God who acts, while at the same time taking seriously those situations where one might expect God to act, but finds that this seems not to happen:

> I saw under the sun that in the place of justice, wickedness was there, and in the place of righteousness, wickedness was there as well. I said in my heart, God will judge the righteous and the wicked, for he has appointed a time for every matter and for every work.

What is not apparent in English is that these two verses are constructed in a chiastic (concentric) fashion which leads from observation of wickedness under the sun to affirmation of justice with God (the whole structure revolving round the observation of wickedness 'there' at the centre):

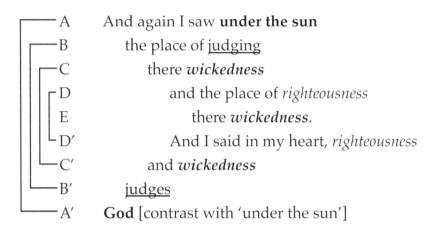

A	And again I saw **under the sun**
B	the place of <u>judging</u>
C	there *wickedness*
D	and the place of *righteousness*
E	there *wickedness*.
D'	And I said in my heart, *righteousness*
C'	and *wickedness*
B'	<u>judges</u>
A'	**God** [contrast with 'under the sun']

These two verses belong together and are supported by 11.9 and 12.14, both of which are also reckoned by many scholars to be later additions. Qohelet, it seems, struggles with maintaining a balance between what he believes about the way God acts and some of the things he observes in the world round about him, under the sun. At times he simply states his belief without understanding just how it all works out in practice.

Thirdly, God is to be worshipped. God acts, according to 3.14, in order that people might fear God (and 'fear' in Hebrew is ambiguous just as it is in English—it may mean 'being afraid' or 'showing due reverence'). 'Fearing God' is mentioned six times in total (3.14; 5.6; 7.18; 8.12, 13; 12.13); and those who are 'good' in God's sight (2.26; 7.26) may be equivalent to those who 'fear' God (7.18; 8.12). In addition, the passage 5.1–7, which instructs the reader concerning appropriate ways to worship, mentions God six times, and the whole book concludes with the words, 'The end of the matter; all has been heard. Fear God, and keep his commandments; for that is the whole duty of everyone. For God will bring every deed into judgment, including every secret thing, whether good or evil.' At least in the canonical form of the book (and I would argue by the author's design) Ecclesiastes ends with a call to worship God. Readers may well come away from Qohelet's exploration of life under the sun with many questions and troubled by some of what they have read. Ecclesiastes does not answer all (or even many of) the questions, it does not seek to ease readers' disquiet about such things as injustice in the world, but in the end it exhorts the reader to worship the God who acts in ways they can never fully comprehend.

So, in light of these comments about the God portrayed in Ecclesiastes, how might we start to answer the questions I raised earlier?

Is it likely that the author of Ecclesiastes intended it to be as ambiguous as I have made out?

In the end we have no way of knowing for sure. Some of the ambiguity may well arise from trying to grapple with an ancient book written in an unusual style of Hebrew. It may be in some cases that a word which seems ambiguous to us was perfectly clear to the first readers. However, there is no doubt in my mind that the book is now ambiguous. I have also become more and more convinced that such ambiguity is actually part of the design of the book and therefore was intended by its author. But why?

Why might the author have produced such an ambiguous book?

Teaching my own students has convinced me of the value of prompting and provoking students to think deeply and develop their own strategies for answering difficult questions (or at times just living with unanswered questions), rather than trying to give them the answers (assuming I could!). One scholar, writing about Ecclesiastes in a book entitled *Wise Teaching, Biblical Wisdom and Educational Ministry*, puts it like this:

> If the author was seeking to transmit clearly and unequivocally his conclusions, why has he chosen words that are so ambiguous and open textured? Is it possible the author did not intend precision in meaning? If not, might that suggest a different way of reading this text? What if [it] does not seek to be simply accepted or assimilated but seeks to arouse contention among reader-learners and thereby stimulate more testing by their own experience, evidence and argument—perhaps even discussion?…Instead of offering reader-learners a conclusion, suppose the text entices reader-learners to join in exploring conflicting views…To expect reader-learners to master the text's doctrine or lessons may be largely to miss the point. The value of the text may be not only the viewpoints espoused within it but the manner in which it seduces reader-learners into reflecting upon life themselves.[38]

If the author of Ecclesiastes was a wise teacher, perhaps he wrote a book that would prompt his students to grapple with the hard questions of life and come up with strategies for answering such questions. But it seems that all this would have been done firmly within a faith context where a God who gives, acts and is to be worshipped was an important part of the equation.

Am I reading Ecclesiastes too much as a child of the postmodern era?
Let the reader decide! Postmodernism is not all bad, nor, I think, are many of
its constituent elements new. People throughout the ages have said and done
things which might today attract the label 'postmodern.' Perhaps in some ways
Qohelet was postmodern before his time. To some extent postmodern society,
including Christian society, is more prepared to tackle the hard questions of
life—and not have to come up with water-tight solutions. Postmodernity has
certainly helped us acknowledge that we do not have all the answers, whether
we are Christians or the cultured despisers of Christianity. Postmodernity,
like Ecclesiastes, helps us open our eyes to the ambiguities and uncertainties
of life. It is in this respect that Ecclesiastes truly is a peculiarly postmodern
book. However, Qohelet's emphasis on a God who gives, acts and is to be
worshipped perhaps fits rather less well with postmodernity's suspicion of
any grand narratives.

*Is the approach to reading I have adopted here appropriate for the reading
of Holy Scripture?*
I do not think we always need to seek for 'the meaning' of a biblical text. Lit-
erature does not always or even usually work like that, and I do not believe
the Bible always or even usually works like that either. For example, many of
Jesus' parables seem to be designed to get listeners (and now readers) thinking for themselves rather than giving a straightforward message. Biblical
narratives engage readers and provoke them to think for themselves about
theological and ethical issues that arise. The psalms can engender very strong
emotions and are probably better 'experienced' than trawled for their 'meaning'—and so on. Biblical texts 'work' in diverse ways, and readers encounter
God in diverse ways as they interact with these texts. Reading the Bible is
not always about what it *means* to the reader. Sometimes it is about what it
does to the reader. Thorough engagement with the text of Ecclesiastes can do
a lot to a reader.

*To what extent ought we as Christians to emphasize certainty over
ambiguity?*
My contention is that the world is a very ambiguous place! Christians should
not bury their heads in the sand, but need to learn to live with ambiguity
and develop Christian strategies for coping with it—and even rejoicing in it!
Nonetheless, many (most?) people do crave certainty in their lives. Ecclesiastes
provides an example of an approach to life which faces its ambiguities head
on and does not hold back from asking the difficult questions, while still hold-
ing firm to belief in a God who gives, acts and is to be worshipped. At times,
though, even this belief in God is fraught with ambiguities and questions.

How might we as Christians cope with a world full of ambiguity and uncertainty?
This takes me to the end of my deliberations and points beyond the scope of my study. But to finish I might just note that the book of Ecclesiastes at least gives some pointers which may head us in the right direction as we continue to grapple with an ambiguous and uncertain world.

- *Realism*
  Ecclesiastes 'tells it like it is.' We have in this book biblical precedent for being brutally honest about our experience of life under the sun and the questions it raises for us. Life is not simple, nor should our Christian understanding of it be simple. Hence my student's observation, 'It seems that in this one book there is more realism about the confusion and ambiguity of life than you could ever expect in the gospel.'

- *There is a God!*
  God *is* a key element in Qohelet's portrayal of the world. Sometimes this is part of the problem, but God is there nonetheless. Ecclesiastes sometimes appeals to people who claim no faith in God because of its realism, as mentioned above. However, it is also a book for people of faith who struggle to understand the world in which they live.

- *God's Gift*
  Accepting what life throws at us as God's gift, rather than demanding things as our right, brings a different perspective on life, even in the midst of uncertainty and ambiguity. In my reading of Ecclesiastes this is one of the key themes which runs as a constant thread throughout the book and is returned to repeatedly in the midst of Qohelet's sometimes painful deliberations.

- *God's Judgment*
  Qohelet (and the book as a whole) holds out that, even when he sees wickedness triumphing, somehow, somewhere God will bring about justice. At times, especially when faced with wickedness where there ought to be righteousness, with oppression where there ought to be respect and dignity, we can but cling on in faith to belief in a God of justice.

- *Worshipping God*
  Even in the midst of struggle turning to God in worship moves our eyes away from ourselves and our own situation. Worship brings us into contact with a God who sees life under the sun from a different perspective. This, of course, is also a key theme in many of the lament Psalms and may be an important element in the book of Job.

- *We See Things 'Under The Sun,' but Things May Look Very Different from God's Perspective*
  Another very important theme in Ecclesiastes relates to the limitations of human knowledge and wisdom. Qohelet sought to be wise, but found that in the end it was beyond him (7.23–24). Qohelet sought to acquire knowledge, but discovered that much that happens under the sun was beyond his ken (8.16–17) let alone what happens 'afterwards' (3.22; 6.12; 8.7; 10.14; 11.2). It is important to learn to accept the necessary limitations that attend our lives under the sun.

- *There is Something of 'Eternity' Within Us, Whatever Precisely That Means*
  Commentators disagree about the interpretation of 3.11, but it seems to suggest that God has placed within us something which encourages us to look beyond life under the sun. The verse in its context seems to indicate that people yearn for something more which in the end only God has access to or control over. Might this correlate with the popular notion of a 'God-shaped void'? (However, one should not read too much into so disputed a verse!)

- *The Whole-Bible Context*
  Scholars, at least until very recently, have tended to insist on the study of the Old Testament (or Hebrew Bible) in its own context, rather than as part of the whole Christian Bible. There is undoubtedly great value in studying Old Testament books and passages within their own contexts before considering them in light of the New Testament—so I tell my students regularly! But as Christians it is crucial for us to take the next step and consider how they function within the Bible as a whole. A common approach to Ecclesiastes in the past was to view it as preparing the way for Jesus because it showed how 'vain' life is without him. While this is very far from the whole story, I do think it has some merit, and is enhanced by the kind of study I have undertaken here. I noted above that Qohelet (and Ecclesiastes as a whole) hints at some possible answers to the questions he raises, but his theological understanding does not permit him to explore them in any depth. Thus, for instance, he affirms that God will judge the righteous and the wicked, he hints ever so tentatively at the possibility of life beyond the grave, and he allows the possibility of there being something other than life 'under the sun.' When we go back to Ecclesiastes in light of the New Testament, having first studied it as much as possible in its Old Testament context, we can see how the gospel does answer some of the questions Qohelet asked.

6

Epilogue

'Ambiguity and unanswerable questions, innocent suffering, joys and tragedies, glimpses of God and brasslike heavens, hope and despair, optimism and pessimism, wrestling and searching…such is the stuff of life and such is the stuff of Job and Ecclesiastes—what a relief!'

I have presented the basic content of this booklet many times now, in a variety of different contexts. The quote above captures a common response among those who have attended these presentations—many people are relieved to find in the Bible a book which is so realistic about the 'ambiguity and unanswerable questions' which attend our experience of this 'vapour-like' life under the sun. Indeed, a number of people have told me that the realism of Ecclesiastes was a key factor in their coming to faith. One of my students tells of an experience she had on placement in a young offenders' institution where she met a young man reading the Bible. He apparently had had no interest in the Bible, which he found to be irrelevant to life as he knew it, until someone directed him to Ecclesiastes. Here he found a biblical book which asked the kind of questions that he asked and took seriously the kind of life issues that he faced.[39]

Here he found a book which asked the kind of questions that he asked and took seriously the kind of life issues that he faced

Ecclesiastes is a book that faces the harsh realities of life head on and refuses to provide nice neat answers. It has throughout its history been interpreted in diverse ways, and I am convinced that it actually invites such diversity of interpretation. In this way the ambiguity of the book captures something of the ambiguity of this harsh life 'under the sun,' the acknowledgment of which is an important aspect of a postmodern worldview. In this respect at least Ecclesiastes is a peculiarly postmodern piece. However, there are also aspects of this book which are rather unpostmodern—constantly in the background for Qohelet, and sometimes in the foreground, is the God who gives, acts and is to be worshipped. It may be that for many readers of the Bible in this postmodern age, the realism of Ecclesiastes and its refusal to provide simplistic, 'trite' answers to the ambiguities of life will facilitate an encounter (or fresh encounter) with such a God in ways which are particularly appropriate for the society in which we now live.

Notes

The author would be pleased to receive any responses to this booklet at d.ingram@stjohns-nottm.ac.uk

1 See the introductory 'Note on Terms' on p 2 in relation to the use of 'Qohelet.'

2 'A vindication of the justice of God in establishing a world where evil exists.' *Chambers English Dictionary* (Edinburgh: W & R Chambers Ltd, 1990).

3 Whybray wrote an article entitled 'Qoheleth, Preacher of Joy' and Cochraine penned 'Joy to the World: The Message of Ecclesiastes.'

4 Walsh's article goes by the title 'Despair as a Theological Virtue in the Spirituality of Ecclesiastes.'

5 Graham Ogden, *Qoheleth* (Sheffield: Sheffield Academic Press, 1987) pp 14–5.

6 Michael V Fox, *Qohelet and His Contradictions* (Sheffield: Sheffield Academic Press, 1989) p 309.

7 Robert Gordis, *Kohelet: the Man and his World. A Study in Ecclesiastes* (3rd edn; New York: KTAV, 1968) p 129.

8 James A Crenshaw, *Ecclesiastes* (London: SCM Press, 1987) p 23.

9 Tremper Longman III, *The Book of Ecclesiastes* (The New International Commentary on the Old Testament; Grand Rapids, MI: Eerdmans, 1997) p 61.

10 Choon-Leong Seow, *Ecclesiastes: A New Translation with Introduction and Commentary* (The Anchor Bible; New York: Doubleday, 1997) p 61.

11 Robin B Salters, 'Exegetical Problems in Qoheleth,' *Irish Biblical Studies* 10 (1988), pp 44–59.

12 R N Whybray, *Ecclesiastes* (Grand Rapids: Eerdmans; London: Marshall, Morgan and Scott, 1989) p 29.

13 James L Crenshaw, 'Qohelet in Current Research,' *HAR* 7 (1983), pp 41–56 (51).

14 Craig G Bartholomew, *Reading Ecclesiastes: Old Testament Exegesis and Hermeneutical Theory* (Analecta Biblica; Rome: Editrice Pontificio Istituto Biblico, 1998) p 269.

15 Gary D Salyer, *Vain Rhetoric: Private Insight and Public Debate in Ecclesiastes* (Sheffield: Sheffield Academic Press, 2001) p 93.

16 Crenshaw, *Ecclesiastes*, p 59.

17 Fox, *Qohelet and His Contradictions*, p 168.

18 Daniel C Fredericks, *Coping with Transience: Ecclesiastes on Brevity in Life* (Sheffield: JSOT Press, 1993) p 14.

19 Kathleen A Farmer, *Proverbs and Ecclesiastes: Who Knows What is Good?* (Grand Rapids: Eerdmans; Edinburgh: The Handsel Press, 1991) pp 142, 146.

20 Thomas Krüger, *Qoheleth* (Hermenia; Minneapolis: Fortress Press, 2004) p 44.

21 Fox, *Qohelet and His Contradictions*, p 170.

22 Michael V Fox, *A Time to Tear Down and A Time to Build Up: A Rereading of Ecclesiastes* (Grand Rapids: Eerdmans, 1999) p 165.

23 Longman, *Ecclesiastes*, p 66.

24 Graham S Ogden and Lynell Zogbo, *A Handbook on Ecclesiastes* (UBS Handbook Series; New York: United Bible Societies, 1997) p 24.

25 Crenshaw, *Ecclesiastes*, p 92.

26 Ogden, *Qoheleth*, p 50.

27 Robert Gordis, *Kohelet: the Man and His World*, pp 228–9.

28 Derek Tidball, *That's Life! Realism and Hope for Today from Ecclesiastes* (Inter-Varsity Press: Leicester, 1989) p 44.

29 Crenshaw, *Ecclesiastes*, p 62.

30 Fox, *Qohelet and His Contradictions*, p 171.

31 Crenshaw, *Ecclesiastes*, p 61.

32 Fox, *Qohelet and His Contradictions*, p 172.

33 N Lohfink, 'The Present & Eternity: Time in Qoheleth,' *Theology Digest* 34 (1987), pp 236–40.

34 Crenshaw, *Ecclesiastes*, p 49.

35 Jacques Ellul, *Reason for Being: A Meditation on Ecclesiastes* (Grand Rapids: Eerdmans, 1990) p 117.

36 In a series of articles in the *Catholic Biblical Quarterly* (vols 30, 42, 45) A G Wright claims to have solved what he calls 'the riddle of the sphinx.'

37 F Delitzsch, *Commentary on the Old Testament in Ten Volumes: Volume VI, Proverbs, Ecclesiastes, Song of Solomon* (Trans by James Martin; Grand Rapids: Eerdmans, 1986 [1872]) p 188.

38 Charles F Melchert, *Wise Teaching: Biblical Wisdom and Educational Ministry* (Harrisburg: Trinity Press International, 1998) pp 118, 122.

39 I note here the comment made by Jo Bailey Wells that 'wisdom offers some ancient insights for a postmodern context, and thus an effective, if unusual, path to faith.'